My Mother's Ghost Scrubs the Floor at 2 a.m.

My Mother's Ghost Scrubs the Floor at 2 a.m.

Robert Okaji

Etchings Press
Indianapolis, Indiana
2021

This publication is made possible by funding provided by the Shaheen College of Arts and Sciences and the Department of English at the University of Indianapolis. Special thanks to the students who judged, edited, designed, and published this chapbook: Lindsey Henderson, Hope Coleman, Adam Lourenco Fernandes, and Pamela Smith.

Published by Etchings Press
1400 E. Hanna Ave.
Indianapolis, Indiana 46227

UNIVERSITY *of*
INDIANAPOLIS

etchings.uindy.edu
www.uindy.edu/cas/english

Printed by IngramSpark

Published in the United States of America

ISBN 978-1-955521-03-1
25 24 23 22 21   1 2 3 4 5

Colophon:
The book interior is set with Alegreya
The cover is set in Letter Gothic and Modula

Cover background image by František G. via Unsplash
Cover design by Adam Lourenco Fernandes
Interior design by Lindsey Henderson

For my mother and father

Table of Contents

Higashi

looking east
through pine branches
at dawn

I feel my mother's last
breath

Bottom Falling

Through that window you see another bird
rising, unlabeled, unwanted, yet noticed.
A limb's last leaf. The boy's hands.
Like the day after your father died,
when temperature didn't register
and heat shallowed through the end.
Still you shivered. Glass. Wind.
Night's body. How to calibrate nothing's
grace? Take notes. Trace its echo. Try.

To the Light Entering the Shack One December Evening

No prayers exit here, nothing
limits you. I never knew
before.

The pear tree's ghost shudders.

Water pools in the depression of its absence.

For decades I have wandered from shadow to
source, longing. Now, at rest,
you come to me and fear
evaporates. I would like to count
the smallest distraction.
I would like to disturb.

You are the name
I whisper
to clouds.

Will you leave if I open the door?

A carnival germinates in my body.

You are not death, but its closest friend.

Darkness parts, folds around you.

I close my eyes and observe.

My Mother's Ghost Sits Next to Me at the Hotel Bar

Blue-tinted and red-mouthed, you light a cigarette
that glows green between your lips and smells of
menthol and old coffins, burnt fruit and days carved

into pale atrocities. I mumble hello, and because
you never speak, order a tulip of double IPA, which the
bartender sets in front of me. Longing to ask someone

in authority to explain the protocol in such matters,
I slide it over, but of course you don't acknowledge
the act. The bartender shrugs and I munch on spiced

corn nuts. I wish I could speak Japanese, I say, or cook
with chopsticks the way you did. We all keep secrets, but
why didn't you share your ability to juggle balls behind

your back sometime before I was thirty? And I still
can't duplicate that pork chili, though my *yaki soba*
approaches yours. You stub out the cigarette and immediately

light another. Those things killed you, I say, but what the hell.
As always, you look in any direction but mine, your face
an empty corsage. What is the half-life of promise, I ask. Why

do my words swallow themselves? Who is the grandfather
of loneliness? Your outline flickers and fades until only a trace
of smoke remains. I think of tea leaves and a Texas noon,

of rice balls and the vacuum between what is and what
could have been, of compromise and stubbornness and love,
then look up at the muted tv, grab your beer, and drink.

Bone Music

But how to reconcile the difference? Consider
drag force, velocity at impact, position,
surface tension. Gravity. I drink more wine
and drift, trying to recall that last conversation,
those few sentences revised in the moment,
exhaled and consumed in passing. It's
likely that fractured ribs lacerated the heart and
lungs or severed major arteries. Sometimes
words evaporate, leaving behind only the faintest
residue. Or they might absorb the ocean's power,
the beauty, the blackness of the deepest
nocturnal canyon or the weight of a dying
high mass star's core, crushing any deliberation,
any attribution, with remorse. Sky above,
earth below, silvered leaves. A shared moon.
This fluttering from great heights. The outward
thrust. The shearing. A fluttering within. Each
morning I acknowledge pain and fear, refleshing
the night's bones phrase by delicate phrase into

numinous forms greater than their divisible
parts, their intractable sums, into bodies and
shapes extracted through a pinholed glimpse,
brief afterthoughts groaned across the opening
blue, saying I was right, I admit inaction, I
confess it all, water, water, I knew too little.

May I Be Familiar

Do we find you in what you've left or where you've gone.

In words you could not form, or forgot long ago.

Missing the pastels, the shades, all nuance.

With moistened hands, I pat rice into a ball and wrap it in seaweed.

By my reckoning, the word *who* no longer implicates.

Ritual accumulates significance in memory.

Forgotten fruit on the sill. A whisper nailed to the wall.

Honor and pride line your earthen home.

Though you never did, I pickle ginger. Make *takuan*.

The transparent house reflects no gaze and contains no one.

Gathering your absence, I coil it around my body.

Mother's Day

The dog is my shadow and I fear his loss. My loss.
I cook for him daily, in hope of retaining him.

Each regret is a thread woven around the oak's branches.
Each day lived is one less to live.

Soon the rabbits will be safe, and the squirrels.
As if they were not. One morning

I'll greet an empty space and walk alone,
toss the ball into the yard, where it will remain.

It is Mother's Day.
Why did I not weep at my mother's grave?

I unravel the threads and place them around the dog.
The wind carries them aloft.

As Blue Fades

Which defines you best, a creaking lid or the light-turned flower?

The coffee's steam or smoke wafting from your hand.

Your bowls color my shelves; I touch them daily.

Sound fills their bodies with memory.

The lighter's click invokes your name.

And the stepping stones to nowhere, your current address.

If the moon could breathe would its breath flavor our nights?

I picture a separate one above your clouded island.

The dissipating blue in filtered light.

Above the coral. Above the waves and ocean floor far below.

Above the space your ashes should share.

Where the boats rise and fall, like chests, like the waning years.

Like a tide carrying me towards yesterday's reef.

Or the black-tailed gull spinning in the updraft.

February 6, 2018

Today every song uncrates a diary of lost dates,
moments cured in precision

and stowed away on a train to the next town,
forever yearning the beyond, around that precious bend.

Or, a funeral for tomorrow, processing the improbable
present. Lights, flickering. The starling's first peep.

All urgency dies. Outside, leaves float in the fog
as I drive away to a finite point.

Now, a whistle mourns the day's broken
surge; never having said goodbye, you drift on.

My Mother's Ghost Scrubs the Floor at 2 a.m.

Even in death she scraps the easy path, choosing thorns and rocks
over blossoms and a groomed walkway. On hands and knees,
scouring the floor with ghost water and a scrub brush made of ancient

thistles, her pale figure flares yellow in the kitchen. *Mom, you don't
have to do this,* I say. *You're dead, and besides, I have a Swiffer
in the garage.* I can almost hear her humming a Ray Charles

song from an album back in the sixties, and I notice that the water
in the transparent bucket remains clear and at the same level no matter
how often she dips into it. What do you say to one who never replies?

We've long splashed through that puddle of contention, and though
wary of repetition's erosive qualities, I resort to ritual, drop a piece of
kombu into a pot of water, bring it to a boil, remove it from the heat,

sift in a handful of dried bonito flakes and a few drops of soy sauce,
stirring it a few times. Then I strain the liquid, spoon in some miso,
add chopped green onion and a few cubes of tofu. I ladle this into two

black and red laquer bowls and set them on opposite sides of the table.
Hours later, the glow from the kitchen has faded, but I fidget and lie
awake, pain pulsing from hip to knee, and wonder if surgery is impending,

whether I should hire someone temporarily to mow the grass. How do
we reconcile reality with emotional drought and flood-swollen
creeks and the inability to draw together those things we desire most?

In the morning the floor is still dirty and the soup is where I'd left it
at the sharp edge separating table from space, another stuttering symbol,
cold and unappetizing, smelling faintly of fish and muddy water.

Better Than Drowning

As clouds leverage sky and the wind scours each night.

Surrounding the spiraling strands. Wherever I am. And am not.

Over the crushing waves, suspended between air and matter.

With the earth in taproots drilled through stone.

Under the layered fog, dampness upon dampness, differing by degree.

I see you where I don't look. You live in the mirror.

The night conceals nothing, not even my guilt.

Not even my pleasure. Nor your smile.

Though no door existed, it closed behind you.

Which is the point of absence, the fulcrum on which I balance.

You turn and join the light, casting no shadow.

Two Cranes on a Snowy Pine (after Hokusai)

Who knows where wing
begins and tree

ends,

which branch shifts
snow, which bears

eternity. This, too, will share

joy,
elusive green

and breath,
with no thought

of flight

and night's
fall.

My Mother's Ghost Knits a Scarf of Chain

When I look up, rust scabs flutter from your clicking
needles, subsuming even the brightest link in this
moon-drenched room. Communion's possibility

perished in that wicker basket, and we hold close our
secrets, looped within circles, joined in these most hidden
stitches. Will you ever detach? I recall losing myself,

stepping from darkness into the white afternoon beyond the movie,
finding only strange faces on a street unraveling from
a wound I'd not yet felt. Now you pull apart the gatherings.

Yesterday's scarf lies incomplete on the invisible shelf,
and tomorrow's tightens uncomfortably around my throat,
even as I read aloud, proposing family life on a scale

we cannot duplicate—in that house lost long ago in a city
I've not yet seen, in a decade before my birth in a pearled
atmosphere of cleansing air into which my body still longs to rise

but can't, tethered in place by love, this terrible, beautiful love.

Pleasure in Absence of Ending (Enso)

Thoughtful, proposing not end, but process.

In this noon's grayness I disclose my need.

Which is a lotus floating in your pond, a clutch of zeros
blooming in moonlight. Last night's missing sleep.

An ending, by definition, concludes.

But what occurs in a circle's body, or infinity's border?

Imprecision acknowledged, I sip wine and gauge distance.

Take comfort in the disorderly.

Starting at the top, the brush moves down and right,
clockwise, then rising in opposition, halts.

Aching, incomplete, I step back.

Some leave a gap; others do not.

Every Wind

Every wind loses itself,
no matter where

it starts. I want
a little piece of you.

No.

I want your atmosphere
bundled in a small rice paper packet
and labeled with strings of new rain
and stepping stones.

I want
the grace of silence
blowing in through the cracked
window, disturbing only
the shadows.

Everywhere I go, bits of me linger,
searching for you.

Grief ages one thread at a time,

lurking like an odor
among the lost
things,

or your breath,
still out there,

drifting.

Ghost, with a Line from Porchia

In my dreams you manifest in a younger form.

If I were to give you life, what could I give you?

Your hands never touched these walls, yet you inhabit them.

As my language inters you, I am absorbed in yours.

Some gifts are simply not proffered, others are released.

My hand retraces your name in both sun and shade.

The rain taps out *regrets, regrets* on the metal roof.

Dim spirit, faint soul. Root-land. Shoal. Mother.

Each visit signals the darkness waiting.

Your battle with language, with silence, invoked.

I stretch the word and weave this dirge for you.

"If I were to give you life, what could I give you?" is from Antono Porchia's *Voices*, translated by W.S. Merwin.

Acknowledgments

Grateful acknowledgment is made to the editors of the publications in which some of these poems first appeared in perhaps slightly different forms:

Into the Void: "Bottom Falling"
The Lake: "Every Wind," "Mother's Day," and "My Mother's Ghost Sits Next to Me at the Hotel Bar"
Shantih: "To the Light Entering the Shack One December Evening"
Gossamer: An Anthology of Contemporary World Poetry: "Bone Music"
On Broken Stones: a Tupelo Press Keepsake: "May I be Familiar"
Underfoot: "As Blue Fades," "Better Than Drowning," and "Ghost, with a Line from Porchia"
North Dakota Quarterly: "February 6, 2018"
Indianapolis Review: "My Mother's Ghost Scrubs the Floor at 2 a.m."
Panoply: "Two Cranes on a Snowy Pine (after Hokusai)" and "My Mother's Ghost Knits a Scarf of Chain"
Posit: "Pleasure in Absence of Ending (Enso)"

About Etchings Press

Etchings Press is a student-run publisher at the University of Indianapolis that runs a post-publication award—the Whirling Prize—as well as an annual publication contest for one poetry chapbook, one prose chapbook, and one novella. On occasion, Etchings Press publishes new chapbooks from previous winners. The press is the new home for the Floodgate Poetry Series. For more information about these contests, the Whirling Prize post-publication award, and the Floodgate Poetry Series, please visit etchings.uindy.edu.

Previous winners and publications:

Poetry
2021: *My Mother's Ghost Scrubs the Floor at 2 a.m.* by Robert Okaji

2020: *Vaginas Need Air* by Tori Grant Welhouse

2019: *As Lovers Always Do* by Marne Wilson

2018: *In the Herald of Improbable Misfortunes* by Robert Campbell

2017: *Uncle Harold's Maxwell House Haggadah* by Danny Caine

2016: *Some Animals* by Kelli Allen

2015: *Velocity of Slugs* by Joey Connelly

2014: *Action at a Distance* by Christopher Petruccelli

Prose

2021: *Bad Man Love Stories* by Curtis VanDonkelaar (fiction)

2020: *Three in the Morning and You Don't Smoke Anymore* by Peter J. Stavros (fiction)

2019: *Dissenting Opinion from the Committee for the Beatitudes*
   by Marc J. Sheehan (fiction)

2018: *The Forsaken* by Chad V. Broughman (fiction)

2017: *Unravelings* by Sarah Cheshire (memoir)

2016: *Pathetic* by Shannon McLeod (essays)

2015: *Ologies* by Chelsea Biondolillo (essays)

2014: *Static: Stories* by Frederick Pelzer (fiction)

Novella

2021: *Miss Alma May Learns to Fight* by Stuart Rose

2020: *Under Black Leaves* by Doug Ramspeck

2019: *Savonne, Not Vonny* by Robin Lee Lovelace

2018: *Edge of the Known Bus Line* by James R. Gapinski

2017: *The Denialist's Almanac of American Plague and Pestilence* by Christopher Mohar

2016: *Followers* by Adam Fleming Petty

Chapbooks from Previous Winners

2020: *Fruit Rot* by James R. Gapinski (fiction)

2016: *#LOVESONG* by Chelsea Biondolillo (microessays with photos and found text)

Robert Okaji is a displaced Texan living in Indiana. A seven-time Pushcart Prize nominee, he holds a BA in history, served without distinction in the U.S. Navy, lived the hand-to-mouth existence of a bookstore owner, worked as a university administrator, and most recently, bagged groceries for a living. He is the author of multiple chapbooks, and his poetry has appeared or is forthcoming in *Taos Journal of International Poetry & Art*, *Boston Review*, *North Dakota Quarterly*, *Panoply*, *Vox Populi*, *Indianapolis Review*, *Book of Matches*, *Slippery Elm* and elsewhere. Visit his blog, O at the Edges, at robertokaji.com.